Contents

A Note About These Stories

Vietnam is a long, narrow country to the south of China. The capital city of Vietnam is Hanoi, in the north. The largest city is Ho Chi Minh City, in the south. Ho Chi Minh City used to be called Saigon.

Vietnam is a very old country. More than 2300 years ago, King Au Duong ruled a kingdom called Au Lac. The Chinese invaded the kingdom and they called the country Nam-Viet. Viet was the name of the people. Nam means south. Later, the country became Viet-nam.

There have been many changes in Vietnam in the last 150 years. The country has been ruled by the French (1858–1945) and the Japanese (1945). Then, Vietnam was divided into two republics – the Democratic Republic of Vietnam in the north and the Republic of South Vietnam. Nguyen Ai Quoc (later called Ho Chi Minh) took power in August 1945. From 1954 to 1974, North and South Vietnam were at war with each other. The Americans fought with the Republic of South Vietnam from 1965 until 1973. The American army left Vietnam in 1973. Vietnam became one country again in 1976.

China brought many ideas and laws to Vietnam. For example, people who wanted to be officials had to study very hard. These scholars, or students, had to pass many difficult exams. The highest officials were mandarins. Mandarins were respected by everyone. People asked mandarins for help. They listened to their words and they obeyed them.

4

The Chinese also brought stories about dragons to Vietnam. Dragons were magic creatures which flew in the air and had many powers. Fish became dragons when they jumped up waterfalls on rivers.

The main religions in Vietnam were Confucianism, Buddhism and Taoism. The people prayed to gods who lived in Heaven. The gods took care of everything. All the gods were ruled by the King of Heaven. People also prayed to the spirits of their ancestors and they prayed to animals and plants.

Some Vietnamese stories are about fairies. These were beautiful spirits who came to live with men and women. Fairies were immortal – they never died.

In very many towns and villages in Vietnam there are pagodas. These beautiful buildings are temples or shrines. People visit shrines, pagodas and temples and they pray to the gods. They remember their ancestors and think about their lives. Most of the temples have incense burners. They are bowls made of metal and they have legs. People light thin sticks of incense and put them in the incense burners. The sweet smoke from the incense carries the peoples' prayers to Heaven.

The Vietnamese people use the words 'Honourable sir' or 'Honourable lady' if they are speaking to someone who is important. They respect people who are wise or old or well-educated. They listen to these peoples' words. The Vietnamese call men 'Uncle' to show their respect.

a waterfall

a tiger

an orange-tree

bees

incense / an incense burner

a fish

a duck

a rooster

a pagoda

a dragon

a toad

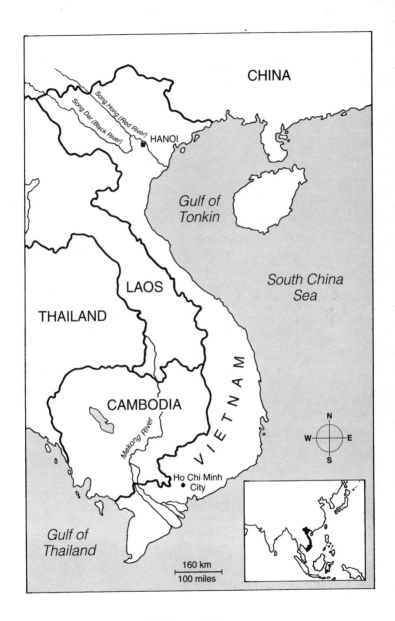

A Map of Vietnam

WHY DUCKS
SLEEP ON ONE LEG

When ducks sleep, they stand on one leg. Do you know why ducks sleep on one leg?

This is what an old Vietnamese legend tells us.

———

At the beginning of time, the gods made four ducks. The ducks lived on a big lake. But the ducks had troubles. Each duck had only one leg. It was very difficult for the ducks to move, on land or on water. On land, they had to hop on one leg. And when they swam on the water, the four ducks went round and round in circles.

'All the other birds have two legs,' said the first duck. 'But we have only one leg. That is wrong! What can we do about it?'

Then the second duck had an idea.

'The gods made us,' he said. 'Will the gods give us another leg? Let's ask them.'

'Where are the gods?' asked the first duck.

'The gods live in Heaven,' said the third duck.

'But where is Heaven?' asked the fourth duck. 'How can we get there?'

'The rooster is very clever,' said the first duck. 'He will know where Heaven is.'

So the ducks went to see the rooster. They told him their idea. The rooster listened carefully.

'You can't go to Heaven!' the rooster said. 'You must go

The ducks told the rooster their idea. The rooster listened carefully.

to the temple. You must pray to the gods. You must ask them for another leg. And you must burn some incense in the temple. If you burn some incense, the smoke will carry your prayers up to Heaven.'

'That's a good idea,' said the ducks.

But the temple was far away, on the other side of the big lake. The ducks had to swim. And each duck had only one leg. So the journey was very, very difficult.

The ducks swam all day. It was nearly dark when they got to the temple. And they were very tired.

They got out of the water and they hopped towards the temple.

Suddenly, the ducks heard a loud voice. The voice was very angry. The ducks were frightened. They stopped and they looked at each other.

'Are the gods angry with us?' they said. 'The gods gave us one leg each. Should we be happy with one leg each?'

But the angry voice was not talking to the ducks. It was talking to someone else.

'Why has the incense burner got eight legs?' the voice asked. 'Incense burners must have four legs. Eight legs are silly! Cut off four of the incense burner's legs immediately!'

When they heard this, the ducks were excited. They wanted four legs! They wanted one leg each. They went quickly into the temple.

Inside the temple, there was a lot of smoke. It was dark. Incense was burning in a large incense burner. The incense burner had eight legs!

In the darkest part of the temple, there were some

wooden gods.

At first, the ducks did not see anybody in the temple. Then they saw an old man with a long grey beard. He was looking at the incense burner. He was worried.

'Remember the rooster's words,' whispered one of the ducks. 'We must burn some incense and we must pray to the gods.'

So the ducks put some incense into the incense burner. Then they prayed to the gods. They asked the gods to give each of them another leg.

'You cannot have another leg!' said the loud voice. Was the voice coming from one of the wooden gods?

'The gods in heaven gave you one leg each,' the voice went on. 'Why aren't you happy with that?'

The ducks were silent for a minute. Then one of them said, 'Oh, Most Important One! All the other birds have two legs, but we have only one. It's very difficult for us to move. We cannot fly as well as the other birds. It is difficult to fly up into the air with one leg. And it is difficult to come down onto the land again with one leg.'

'The gods did not want you to fly,' said the voice. 'Did you think of that?'

'But we cannot run, or walk,' the duck went on. 'We have to hop everywhere. And when we swim on the water, we go round and round in circles! All the other birds laugh at us.'

'I understand,' said the voice. It was kinder now. 'But I cannot do anything about your legs.'

'Excuse me, Most Important One,' said the duck. 'The

*The ducks asked the gods to
give each of them another leg.*

incense burner has eight legs. Can we have four of the incense burner's legs?'

The ducks heard a sound. It came from the darkest part of the temple. It was the sound of somebody laughing!

Then the voice said, 'You are clever and brave. I will give you each another leg. You can take four legs from the incense burner. But be careful! The legs are made of gold.'

The ducks were very happy. 'Oh, we will be careful, we will!' they said. 'We promise. We will take care of the gold legs.'

Then the ducks burnt more incense and thanked the god.

The old man with the beard cut four legs from the incense burner. The ducks watched him. They were very excited. Then each duck attached a leg to its body. And the ducks walked out of the temple. They did not have to hop!

Night had come. The moon was shining brightly. The ducks swam quickly across the lake.

'Two legs are wonderful!' one of the ducks said. 'We can swim much quicker now.'

Soon it was time to sleep.

'We must remember our promise to the god,' one of the ducks said.

'We remember,' the other ducks said. And they held their legs of gold up, close to their bodies.

———

Every night, the four ducks did the same thing. When

their children were born, each little duck had two legs. But when they went to sleep, all the ducks held one leg up, close to their bodies. And from that time, all ducks have slept on one leg!

THE KING OF HEAVEN'S UNCLE

A very long time ago, life on the Earth was good. Then, suddenly, there was a terrible drought. Month after month, there was no rain. And there were no clouds in the sky. The land was no longer green and wet. The land was brown and dry. The trees began to die. The hot sun shone all day. The water in the lakes and rivers disappeared. Animals became sick and they died. The Earth was dying.

A little brown toad lived on the edge of a lake. Every day, the toad watched the sun burning the land.

'If there is no rain soon, I will die,' thought the little animal. 'And everything around me will die too. But what can I do?'

The toad looked up. He could not see see any clouds. There was only blue sky.

'Why doesn't the King of Heaven help us?' thought the toad. 'Is he too far away? Can't he see? Everything on earth is dying.'

The toad decided to do something.

'I'll go and see the King of Heaven myself!' he said. 'The Earth must have rain, or everything will die.'

When the night came, the Earth was cooler. The toad began his journey to Heaven. He met many sick and dying animals on his journey.

'Where are you going, toad?' some monkeys asked him.

'I'm going to see the King of Heaven,' replied the toad. 'I'm going to tell him to send rain. The animals and trees and plants are dying.'

'We cannot come with you,' said the monkeys. 'We have no food to eat. We have no water to drink. We are too weak to travel. We must stay here. Good luck, toad!'

The toad walked on quickly. Soon he heard some bees. They were flying around a tree.

'Where are you going, toad?' asked the bees.

'I'm going to see the King of Heaven,' said the toad. 'I'm going to tell him to send rain.'

'We'll come with you,' said the bees.

So the bees flew along beside him. They travelled with the toad on his journey to Heaven.

An hour later, the travellers saw a rooster. He was walking round and round on the dry ground.

'Where are you going, toad?' the rooster asked.

The toad told him.

The rooster listened carefully. Then he said, 'I'll go with you. I'm a strong bird. I've lived through many droughts. And I'm very angry! All my wives are sick. And our children are dying because there is no food for them.'

So the rooster travelled with the bees and the toad. They travelled together on their journey to Heaven.

Later, the travellers saw a tiger.

'Don't be afraid,' the tiger said. 'I'm very hungry. But I never eat animals who are sick or dying. I have heard about your journey. I want to go with you.'

'All right,' said the toad. 'You can come with us.'

So the tiger travelled with the bees, the rooster and the toad. They travelled together on their journey to Heaven.

*The tiger, the bees, the rooster and the toad travelled
together on their journey to Heaven.*

At last, they came to the edge of the sea. Suddenly, the wind picked up the travellers. It carried them up into the dark sky. Then they climbed from star to star. After a long time, they reached the gates of Heaven.

The travellers opened the gates and they went up some steps. Then they went through many beautiful buildings and gardens.

'Heaven is very big,' said the rooster. 'Which way shall we go now?'

Suddenly, they heard the sounds of laughter and singing. The sounds came from a large building.

'Well, someone is happy,' said the toad. 'Stay here,' he told the others. 'I'll call you soon.'

The toad jumped up some steps and he went into the large building. Soon he was in a large, beautiful room. Musicians were playing. People were dancing and singing. Other people were sitting at tables. They were eating and drinking. Everyone was very happy.

At one end of the room, the King of Heaven was sitting in a large gold chair. There was a chess-board in front of him. The king was playing a game of chess.

Suddenly, the toad was very angry.

'Why are all these people happy?' he thought. 'Why are they singing and dancing? Everything on the Earth is dying!'

The toad jumped across the floor. Then he jumped onto the king's chess-board.

The King of Heaven looked at the little brown toad. The king's face went red. He was very angry. But the toad was not afraid.

'What are you doing, you ugly little toad!' the king shouted.

'Excuse me, Majesty,' the toad began. 'I have come to ask—'

'Guards!' shouted the king.

Ten strong, fierce men ran into the room. They were soldiers. They held large swords in their hands. They were the king's guards!

But the toad moved quickly. He jumped from the chessboard and he ran to the door.

'Bees!' the toad cried.

Immediately, the bees flew into the room. They flew inside the soldiers' clothes. They flew into the soldiers' hair. They began to sting the men.

There were cries of 'Stop!' and 'Help!' The guards threw down their swords and they screamed with pain. They began to pull off their clothes.

'Dogs!' shouted the king. 'Bring in the dogs!'

Immediately, twenty big dogs ran into the room. They had large, sharp teeth.

But the toad was not afraid.

'Tiger!' he cried loudly.

And the tiger ran into the room. His teeth were larger and sharper than the dogs' teeth.

The dogs were very frightened. They turned and they quickly ran away.

The noise was terrible. The King of Heaven was shouting angrily.

'Thunder! Lightning!' he shouted.

Two gods, Thunder and Lightning, ran into the room. They made a terrible noise too!

But the toad was not afraid. He jumped back onto the chess-board.

'Rooster!' the toad shouted.

The rooster flew into the room. His cries were louder than the noise of Thunder and Lightning!

The king held up his hands.

'Stop! Stop!' he cried. 'Stop this terrible noise!' And suddenly, everything was quiet.

The King of Heaven looked at the toad.

'What do you want, toad?' he asked.

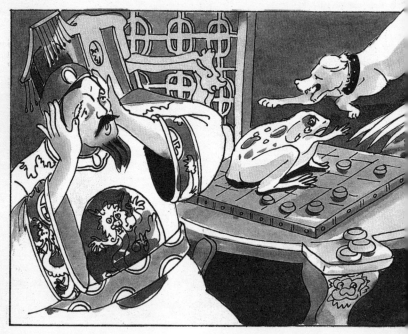

'Stop this terrible noise!' cried the King of Heaven.

'Majesty,' said the little toad politely. 'We have come from the Earth to ask for your help. There has been no rain for many months. All the trees and plants are dying. The rivers and lakes are dry. There is nothing to eat and there is nothing to drink. Many animals have died. Many animals wanted to travel with us, but they were too weak. Majesty, you must give us rain.'

The king was surprised. 'That is terrible news!' he said. 'Yes, Uncle, you must have rain immediately.'

The King of Heaven called the toad 'Uncle', because he respected the brave little animal.

The king spoke to the gods, Thunder and Lightning. He was very angry with them.

'Have you forgotten to do your work?' he said. 'Did you forget to send rain to the Earth?'

Then the king looked at the toad.

'Uncle,' he said, 'Thunder and Lightning are always fighting. They both want to be the most powerful god. Each god wants to make a louder noise than the other. They forget why they make their noise. Thunder and Lightning make storms. People on the Earth hear their noise. Then they stay in their houses and they wait for the rain to fall.'

He turned to the two gods again.

'Why haven't you made any storms?' he said. 'Give rain to the Earth now or I will take away your powers!'

'Yes, yes, Majesty!' cried Thunder.

Thunder clapped his hands together. Lightning threw his sudden bright light across the sky. Then came the sound of rain.

The toad, the bees, the tiger and the rooster ran to the door. They looked down. And they saw rain falling onto the Earth below.

The toad spoke to the King of Heaven.

'Thank you, Majesty,' he said.

The king smiled. 'Uncle,' he said, 'when you need rain, call me. When I hear your voice, I'll tell the gods to send rain to the Earth.'

'Thank you,' said the toad. 'I will always remember your words.'

——

Soon, the toad and his friends returned to the Earth. And soon, everything was green and wet again. The rivers and lakes were full of water. Life on the Earth was good again.

After that, Heaven always heard the voice of the toad. And the gods sent rain to the Earth. But the Vietnamese people have not forgotten the toad's brave journey. Now, when the rain comes after a drought, they think of the toad.

'The King of Heaven has heard the toad's voice,' they say. 'He has sent the rain because the toad is the King of Heaven's uncle.'

THE SCHOLAR'S JOURNEY

There was once a poor young scholar. He worked very hard. He never went out to enjoy himself. He studied his books for many hours every day. But his studying did not bring him success.

The scholar wanted to be a government official. But first, he had to pass some examinations. He had taken the examinations twice. But he had failed the examinations each time.

'I don't understand,' he said to himself. 'Other young men don't study as much I do. But they pass their examinations. They have good luck. They become rich and important. And many of these young men have beautiful wives. But no young woman wants to marry me. Why not? I am not handsome, but I am not ugly.'

The scholar was very unhappy. But what could he do! He sat down and he thought. He did not know what to do.

One day he had an idea. 'I will go to the temple,' he thought. 'I will pray to the gods. The gods will help me.'

So he went to the temple and he prayed. He went to the temple every day for many weeks. But nothing changed. So the young man sat down and he thought again. He remembered a wise old man.

The old man had been a famous scholar. And he had been a government official. But now he lived alone, at the top of a hill.

The next day, the young scholar went to see the wise

old man. The old man lived in a little house on the hill. He had white hair and a long white beard. He listened carefully to the young scholar.

After a few minutes, the old man said, 'I can't help you. You must go up into the high mountains. The gods live there. They will listen to you. The gods can help you.'

'Thank you,' said the scholar. And he walked on over the hills, towards the high mountains.

———

Night came. The scholar stopped at a small hut in a forest. He knocked on the door. A man opened the door. He was a woodcutter. He cut down trees in the forest.

'Can I sleep here tonight?' asked the young scholar. 'I'm travelling to the high mountains.'

'Yes, please come inside,' said the woodcutter. 'I live here with my daughter. We don't have many visitors.'

The woodcutter gave the scholar something to eat and something to drink. Then he asked, 'Why are you travelling up to the high mountains?'

The young scholar told his story to the woodcutter.

'I want the gods to help me,' he said. 'I have failed my examinations. I cannot find a wife. I'm not handsome, but—'

The scholar stopped speaking. He was very sad.

'My daughter has troubles too,' said the woodcutter kindly. 'She cannot speak and she cannot hear. Will you ask the gods to help my daughter?'

'Yes, I will do that,' said the young man.

———

Very early the next morning, the young scholar left the woodcutter's hut. All day, he walked down into valleys and up over hills. Then it was evening again.

The scholar walked to a house in a valley. There were many orange trees growing round the house. The man who lived there – an orange-grower – gave the scholar some food.

'Please sleep here tonight,' the man said.

'Thank you,' said the scholar. 'I'm travelling to the high mountains.' And again, he told his story.

'Will you ask the gods to help me?' asked the orange-grower. 'Many oranges grow on the trees at the front of my house. But no oranges grow on the trees behind the house.'

'That is very strange,' said the young scholar.

'Yes, it is strange,' agreed the orange-grower. 'I am very worried. If oranges will not grow on *all* my trees, I will have to sell my land.'

'I will ask the gods to help you,' said the scholar.

The next morning, the young scholar left the orange-grower's house. Soon he came to a deep river. There was a high waterfall on the river. There was no bridge and there was no boat.

'How can I get across this river?' the scholar asked himself.

Then he saw a huge golden fish. It was jumping up into the waterfall. Again and again, the golden fish jumped. But again and again, it fell back into the river.

The young man understood.

'The golden fish wants to become a dragon,' he

'If oranges will not grow on all my trees,
I will have to sell my land.'

thought. 'All fish want to become dragons. But first, they have to jump to the top of a waterfall. It is difficult for the fish to jump. And it is difficult for me to pass my examinations.'

At last, the fish stopped jumping. It swam to the edge of the river and it looked up at the young scholar.

'I want to get over the waterfall,' the fish said sadly. 'But I cannot jump high enough. I'll never become a dragon.'

'I have troubles too,' said the young man. 'I want to pass my examinations, but I always fail them.'

Then he had an idea. 'I'm going to the place where the gods live,' he said. 'I'm going to ask the gods to help me. And I'm going to ask them to help two other people. Shall I ask the gods to help you? They can help you to climb the waterfall.'

'Oh, yes!' said the fish.

'All right,' said the young man. 'But first, I want your help. Can you carry me across this river?'

'Yes, I can,' said the fish.

Carefully, the young scholar climbed onto the fish's back. Then the fish swam across the river.

'Thank you,' said the young scholar.

———

The young scholar continued his journey. Soon, he came to the highest mountain. He started to climb. Up and up he went.

When he reached the top of the highest mountain, he stood quietly. The scholar began to pray to the gods. Then suddenly, three gods were standing in front of him.

The scholar told them about the golden fish.

'The fish has a piece of jade in its mouth,' said the first god. 'This stone is too heavy. Tell the fish to remove the stone. Then the fish will be able to fly over the waterfall. The fish will become a dragon.'

'Thank you,' said the young scholar. Then he told the gods about the orange-grower's troubles.

The second god spoke.

'There are two jars in the ground behind the man's house,' he said. 'The jars are full of gold. Tell the orange-grower to take the jars out of the ground. Then his oranges will grow.'

The young scholar thanked the god. Then he said, 'There is a young woman. She is the daughter of a wood-cutter. She is deaf and she cannot speak. Can you help her too?'

The third god spoke.

'She will speak and hear when she meets her husband,' he said.

Then suddenly, the three gods had gone.

'I did not ask them about my own troubles,' the young man said to himself. But he was pleased. Now he could help the fish, the orange-grower and the woodcutter's daughter.

He started on his long journey home.

———

When he reached the river, the golden fish was waiting.

'You must take that heavy piece of jade out of your mouth,' the scholar said. 'Then you will be able to fly over the waterfall.'

The big fish opened its mouth, and the stone fell out.

'Please take the piece of jade,' the fish said to the young man. And he carried the scholar across the river.

Then the golden fish began to jump high up into the waterfall. Each jump was higher than the jump before. Suddenly, the fish flew over the top of the waterfall! The fish had become a dragon!

The young scholar walked up onto hills and down into valleys. In the evening, he came to the orange-grower's house.

The orange-grower was waiting for him.

'Did you tell the gods about my orange trees?' the orange-grower asked.

'There are two jars of gold buried in the ground behind your house,' the scholar told him. 'Take the jars out of the ground. Then oranges will grow on all your trees.'

Immediately, the man began to dig behind his house. Soon, he found the jars of gold. He took them out of the ground. Suddenly, oranges started to grow on the trees behind the house.

'This is wonderful!' the orange-grower said to the young man. 'Please take one of the jars of gold.'

The scholar was very happy. He slept at the orange-grower's house that night. In the morning, he started his journey again.

When he got to the woodcutter's hut, he saw the wood-cutter's daughter. She was waiting for him. And when she saw the young scholar, she smiled. Then she spoke to him!

Suddenly, the fish flew over the top of the waterfall.

'Will you eat a meal with us?' she asked.

'Yes, please,' the young man replied.

The young woman smiled again.

Then the woodcutter came out of the hut.

'This is wonderful!' he cried. 'My daughter can speak and hear. Young man, will you marry my daughter?'

The two young people looked at each other.

'Yes,' said the young scholar. He smiled at the girl and she smiled at him. 'I want to marry her very much,' he said.

'And I want to marry this young man!' said the wood-cutter's daughter.

The young scholar was very pleased. 'I'm going to marry a beautiful girl,' he thought. 'And I've got a jar of gold too.'

He looked at the piece of jade in his hand.

'My troubles are finished,' he said. 'I shall have good luck now.'

And he was right. He took his examinations again. And he passed them. He became a government official.

A few years later, he was a rich and important man. But he never forgot his journey to the mountains. He often spoke about it.

'I learnt something on my journey,' he said. 'Helping other people brings good luck!'

The young scholar smiled at the girl and she smiled at him.

THE TWO IMMORTALS

Many hundreds of years ago, there was a clever young scholar called Tu Uyen. He was quiet and gentle, and he was handsome. Many young women wanted to marry him. But Tu Uyen did not want to get married. He wanted to study his books. He was studying for his examinations.

'One day, I'll be an important government official,' he said to himself. 'One day, I'll be a mandarin.'

———

One morning, the young scholar was reading a book. Suddenly, he looked out of his window.

'What a beautiful day,' he said to himself. 'I will walk in the fields today.'

Tu Uyen put down his book and he went outside. It was a beautiful morning. The sun was shining brightly. The rice fields were green. The river was silver. White and yellow flowers moved in the gentle wind. The air was fresh and the sun was warm. Tu Uyen heard the sounds of birds and insects everywhere.

He walked all day. At last, it began to get dark. Tu Uyen turned and started to walk home. He walked past a beautiful old pagoda. Outside this shrine, there was a peach tree. The scholar saw a young woman standing by the tree. Her hair was black and soft. Her long dress was made of lovely pink silk. It was the colour of the peach flowers.

'What a beautiful young woman,' thought Tu Uyen.

The scholar saw a young woman standing by the tree.

'She is the loveliest young woman I have ever seen!'

The young woman waited for the scholar to speak.

At last, Tu Uyen said, 'Good evening.'

'Good evening,' the young woman replied. Her voice was soft and lovely.

At that moment, Tu Uyen fell in love.

'Honourable lady,' he said. 'It is getting dark and you are alone. Shall I walk home with you?'

'Thank you, sir,' she replied. 'That is very kind of you.'

The two young people walked together. Tu Uyen and the beautiful young woman spoke softly. They spoke about the trees and the flowers.

Night came. Soon, the moon was shining in the dark sky. The two young people walked on.

'Is this a dream?' Tu Uyen asked himself. 'If it is a dream, I don't want to wake up.'

'Honourable lady, where do you live?' Tu Uyen asked. He turned towards her.

But the beautiful young woman had gone! One moment, she was there. The next moment she had gone!

'She was a fairy,' thought Tu Uyen.

———

The next day, Tu Uyen went back to the old pagoda. But the young woman was not there. She was not by the peach tree. Day after day, Tu Uyen looked for the young woman. But he did not find her.

Tu Uyen could not forget the young woman. He thought about her all day and all night. He could not eat or sleep. He could not study his books. He became ill.

'If I don't see her again soon, I shall die,' he thought.

———

One night, Tu Uyen had a dream. In this dream, he saw an old man.

'Go to the East Bridge on the river,' the old man said. 'There you will see the lady from the pagoda.'

The next morning, Tu Uyen woke up early. He ran to the East Bridge. But no one was there. He waited. But the young woman did not come.

Later that morning, an old man came to the bridge. He had a little table with many things on it. Tu Uyen went to see what the old man was selling.

On the table, there was a picture of the fairy!

'I want to buy that picture! I must have that picture,' Tu Uyen said. He put some money into the old man's hand. Then he took the picture and he ran home.

All that day, Tu Uyen looked at the picture. Sometimes he talked to it.

In the evening, he spoke to his servant.

'A visitor is coming to dinner,' he said.

The servant put two bowls on the table. Tu Uyen put the picture of the beautiful young woman on one side of the table. He sat down at the other side. First, he put some food in the young woman's bowl. Then, he put some food in his own bowl. He began to eat.

After this, Tu Uyen ate with the picture every evening.

———

One evening, the scholar was eating his dinner and looking at the picture. Suddenly, the beautiful fairy began to

First, he put some food in the young woman's bowl. Then, he put some food in his own bowl.

smile. Then, she walked out of the picture and stood in front of him!

'Honourable sir,' she said. 'My name is Giang Kieu. I have come to live with you. I will be your wife. The Fairy Queen has sent me.'

Tu Uyen was very, very pleased. 'I'm the happiest man in the world!' he said.

So, Tu Uyen and Giang Kieu got married. The young scholar gave his new wife many presents.

'I love you very much,' he told her. 'Everyone in the world must know this!'

The wedding celebrations went on for many days. Tu Uyen invited many friends to meet his beautiful wife. He was very happy. Before he married Giang Kieu, only his books made him happy. Now he had a beautiful wife!

But one morning, Giang Kieu said, 'Husband, you must study your books now.'

'But I don't want to study now,' he replied.

'Husband,' she repeated. 'Why did you see me by the peach tree? Do you know?'

'No,' he said. 'Why did I see you there?'

'You were clever and you worked hard,' she replied. 'So the Fairy Queen sent me here. One day you will be a mandarin, Tu Uyen. But you must study your books again. If you don't study, I shall leave you.'

Tu Uyen was afraid. He did not want his wife to leave. So he tried to study again. It was hard work. He had for-gotten how to study.

'Why do I have to work?' he asked himself. 'I have

everything now. I have a beautiful wife and good friends.'

So every day and every night, he talked and he drank with his friends. He did not study.

One evening, Tu Uyen returned to his house very late. Giang Kieu was waiting for him. She was holding the empty picture. She was very angry.

'Husband!' she said. 'I have asked you to study. But you have been drinking with your friends. You do not listen to me!'

She put the empty picture against the wall. Then she walked back into the picture.

'No!' cried Tu Uyen.

But it was too late! His wife was now in the picture. And the face in the picture did not move.

Tu Uyen was very unhappy.

'Please, please, dear wife!' he cried. 'Please return to me. I will study my books again. I promise! I will study every day.'

But the picture did not move. Giang Kieu could not hear him.

'I will kill myself!' Tu Uyen said to the picture.

But Giang Kieu did not come back.

Finally, the scholar opened his books. He studied for seven days. He worked very hard. On the eighth day, Giang Kieu walked out of the picture again.

'My wife!' Tu Uyen cried happily. 'You've come back to me!'

'If I leave you again, I will never come back,' Giang Kieu said sadly.

'You will not leave me again,' said Tu Uyen. 'I promise you. I will study every day. I will work hard.'

And the scholar did work hard. At the end of the year, he took his examinations and he passed them.

———

Tu Uyen and Giang Kieu lived together very happily. Many years later, Tu Uyen became a mandarin. And Giang Kieu had a son. They named him Tran Nhi.

One day, a woman from the village came to see Tu Uyen. She was very sad.

'Honourable sir,' she said. 'My baby has died. Please, can I come and take care of your son?'

Tu Uyen spoke to the woman kindly.

'Yes,' he said. 'You can be our son's nurse.'

The woman was a good nurse. She took care of Tran Nhi very well.

When the boy was a year old, Tu Uyen and Giang Kieu invited many important people to their house.

'Come to Tran Nhi's birthday celebrations,' they said.

Tu Uyen loved his son very much. 'One day, Tran Nhi will be a mandarin too,' he told everyone.

That evening, after the visitors had gone home, Tu Uyen and Giang Kieu were talking quietly. Suddenly, they heard strange and beautiful music. It was music from another world.

'What is this strange music?' asked Tu Uyen. 'What is happening?'

Giang Kieu held her husband's hand and she spoke sadly.

'One day, Tran Nhi will be a mandarin too,'
he told everyone.

'Tu Uyen,' she said. 'I am an immortal. I shall never die. But my life on Earth has ended. The Fairy Queen is calling me. Come with me, Tu Uyen! You will be immortal too. We will be together forever.'

'But, our son—' Tu Uyen began.

'Tran Nhi's nurse will take care of him,' Giang Kieu said. 'She loves him and he loves her. One day, we'll come back for him. Then we will all live together in Heaven.'

So Tu Uyen prayed to the gods. Then he kissed his son. Tu Uyen held his wife's hand and they left their house together.

Outside the house, two beautiful white birds were waiting for them.

Tu Uyen and Giang Kieu got onto the backs of the birds. Again, they heard the strange music. And they quickly flew up into the sky.

43

The villagers heard the music too. They came out of their houses and they looked up at the sky. They saw Tu Uyen and Giang Kieu. They were now bright stars. They were immortal!

'Our honourable mandarin has left us,' one villager said. 'Tu Uyen and Giang Kieu are now in Heaven.' Then all the villagers prayed to the gods.

Afterwards, the villagers built a temple. They built it for Tu Uyen.

Today, Tu Uyen's village is the city of Hanoi. There are many temples in Hanoi. Is one of them Tu Uyen's temple?

THE CLEVER WIFE

Hai and Ba were the sons of a farmer. Hai was older than his brother, Ba. When their father died, Hai owned the farm. He owned it because he was the eldest brother.

The farm was very successful. It had many good, wet fields. Hai kept the best of these fields for himself. He gave Ba some fields at the edge of the farm. But these fields were dry and there were many stones in them.

Ba worked in his fields from early morning until late evening. But the ground was bad. Ba could not grow enough food for his family.

Finally, Ba went to see his brother.

'I cannot grow enough rice for my family,' Ba said to his brother. 'Can I work on your farm too, Hai?'

'Ba is a good worker,' thought Hai. 'He will help me make money.'

'All right, Brother,' Hai agreed. 'But you must work very hard.'

After that, Ba worked in Hai's fields every day. And he worked very hard. In the evenings, he worked in his own fields. At last, he could feed his family.

Ba's life was difficult. Hai's life was very different. Hai lived in a beautiful house. He had expensive furniture. He had many friends and he was kind to them. He invited them to dinner. He gave them rice wine and good food. He gave them expensive presents. When they needed money, Hai gave them some.

*The ground was bad. Ba could not grow enough
food for his family.*

One day, Hai's wife spoke to him.

'Why don't you help your brother?' she said. 'Pay Ba more money. Or give Ba half of the farm. He needs help.'

'I'm the eldest son,' said Hai. 'The land is mine. Ba can feed his family now.'

'But you give many things to your friends,' his wife said. 'Why can't you give things to Ba? He is your brother.'

'My friends—' began Hai.

'Your friends are bees round a jar of honey,' said his wife. 'And you are the jar of honey! Will they help you, if you are in trouble?'

'Yes, my friends will help me,' said Hai. 'Now stop talking about my brother.'

But that day something happened. And Hai's wife had an idea.

'Hai is wrong,' she said to herself. 'But he will learn.'

———

When Hai came home that evening, his wife ran to the door.

'Oh, Husband!' she cried. 'Something terrible has happened!'

'What is it?' said Hai. 'What is wrong?'

'I've killed somebody!' she said.

'Killed somebody?' repeated Hai. He could not believe this.

'Yes!' said his wife. 'What shall I do?'

Suddenly, Hai was afraid. 'This is terrible!' he cried.

'I'm sorry, I—' Hai's wife began. She had tears in her eyes.

'What happened? What happened?' said Hai quickly.

'A beggar came to the door,' his wife said. 'He wanted some food. I went to the kitchen. I went to get him some soup. When I came back, he was stealing a jar. I was very angry. I hit him with a brush. I killed him!'

'Where is the beggar?' asked Hai.

'I put him in a blanket,' said his wife. 'He's in the kitchen. Quickly! We must bury him tonight.'

'Where shall we bury him?' Hai asked.

'Dig a hole in a field,' said his wife. 'Bury him there. But don't do it alone. The body is very heavy. Go to one of your friends. Ask a friend to help you.'

'Yes!' said Hai. 'Yes, I'll ask my best friend. I'll ask him immediately.'

Hai left his house quickly. He went to his best friend's house. He told his friend the bad news.

'You must help me!' Hai said.

'Ah, Hai. I'm sorry,' said the friend. 'I can't help you. I have hurt my back. I hurt it yesterday. I can't lift heavy things today.'

Hai went to another friend's house.

'Come in, Hai. Please sit down,' said the friend. 'Do you want a cup of rice wine?'

'Thank you,' said Hai. He sat down and his friend gave him a cup of wine. Then Hai told his friend about the dead beggar.

'You must help me!' Hai said.

Hai's friend spoke quickly. 'I can't help you, Hai,' he said. 'My uncle is very ill. I must visit him tonight. I must go out now.'

'I did not know about your uncle,' said Hai.

'Oh yes, he's very ill,' said his friend. 'I'm sorry, Hai.'

Hai went to another friend, and another, and another. None of his friends could help him. Some of them were busy. Some of them were ill.

Hai was worried and afraid. It was very late when he went home.

'None of my friends will help me,' he told his wife. 'You were right! What shall I do?'

'You must go and ask Ba to help,' his wife said. 'Ba will help. Go quickly, Hai! It will soon be morning.'

'Will Ba help me?' asked Hai. 'I haven't been kind to Ba. He works very hard. I don't pay him much money. I gave him the dry fields—'

'Ba is your brother,' said Hai's wife. 'He will come!'

And she was right. Ba came immediately.

'I'll help you, Hai,' he said. 'We must work quickly.'

The two brothers worked together. Quickly, they buried the heavy body in one of Hai's fields.

———

The next morning, Hai and Ba were sitting in the kitchen of Hai's house. They were drinking hot tea.

Suddenly, somebody knocked on the door. Hai opened the door. Two guards were standing outside the house.

'Come with us!' one of the guards said to Hai. 'The mandarin wants to see you.'

Hai was afraid. He went with the two guards. His brother went with them too.

49

When they arrived at the mandarin's house, Hai was very surprised. All his friends were there!

The mandarin spoke to Hai.

'A man has been killed,' he said. 'These people told me about it. You killed the man. And you buried his body. You will be punished! Now, take me to the body.'

Hai, Ba, the guards, the mandarin and Hai's friends walked to Hai's farm. Hai took everyone to the field where he and Ba had buried the body.

'The body is here,' he said.

'Dig up the body,' said the mandarin.

Hai and Ba began to dig. Soon, they found the blanket.

'The body is in the blanket,' said Hai.

The guards took the blanket from the ground. They opened it. Inside the blanket, they found the body of a big black dog!

Hai was very surprised. 'This is my dog!' he said. 'My old dog is dead!'

'What is happening?' the mandarin said angrily.

Hai's friends did not speak. They did not understand what had happened.

But Hai's wife walked up to the mandarin.

'Honourable sir,' she said. 'I will tell you everything.'

She pointed at the men who were standing in the field. 'These are my husband's friends,' she said. 'My husband was kind to his friends. But he was not kind to Ba, his brother.

'Hai was wrong!' Hai's wife went on. 'Ba is a good man. He always helps his family. When everything is good,

The guards took the blanket from the ground.

these men are my husband's friends. But when there is trouble, they are not his friends. I wanted Hai to learn this.

'Our dog died yesterday,' Hai's wife said. 'And I had an idea—'

She stopped speaking. She stopped speaking because the mandarin had started to laugh. He laughed and laughed. For a minute, the mandarin could not speak.

Then he said, 'You are very clever. Your husband has learnt about his friends. And he has learnt about himself too.'

Hai put his arms around his brother.

'I was wrong, Ba,' he said. 'I'm sorry. I was not kind to you. But now, I will give you half of the farm.'

And after that, the brothers helped each other. They helped each other in the good times and in the bad times.

THE WONDERFUL PLANT

One afternoon, a young man walked into a village. He had travelled a long way. His clothes were torn and dirty. And he was hungry. He had not eaten for two days.

The young man looked around him. He smiled. He was happy. There were good, green rice fields. There were many ducks swimming on the river.

The young man was very tired, but he smiled. He was a handsome young man and he had a happy smile. He smiled at everyone who passed him.

Some of the villagers came to speak to the traveller.

'Why are you smiling?' one of the villagers asked.

'I have a secret!' the traveller said.

'What is your secret?' asked another villager.

'I know about a wonderful plant,' the traveller said. 'This plant can feed all the people in a town. It can feed all the people in a city. If you have this plant, you do not need anything else.'

'That is wonderful!' the villagers thought. 'This young man found the wonderful plant on his travels.'

There was a rich man who lived in the village. He heard about the young traveller and the wonderful plant.

'I must meet this traveller,' the rich man thought.

He spoke to one of the villagers. 'Tell the young man to come to my house,' he said.

———

Early in the evening, the young man came to the rich

'Why are you smiling?' one of the villagers asked.

man's house. When he went into the house, the traveller smelled some food. Somebody was cooking the rich man's dinner. It was a good smell. The young man was very hungry!

'Come in, come in!' said the rich man. 'I have heard about you. You know about a wonderful plant. A plant which can feed everybody in a town or a city. Is that right?'

'Yes, that's right,' said the young man.

The rich man was excited. 'Will you have some dinner with me?' he asked. 'Then we can talk about your wonderful plant.'

'Thank you,' said the young man. 'I will eat with you. And I will tell you about the wonderful plant.'

The food was very good. The young man ate a lot of it.

'Please have some more,' said the rich man.

'Thank you,' said the traveller. And he ate some more of the good food.

'Would you like some rice wine?' the rich man asked.

'Thank you,' said the young man.

The rich man gave the traveller more and more food and wine. At last, the young man stopped eating.

'That was a wonderful meal,' he said. 'Thank you.'

'Now, tell me about the wonderful plant,' said the rich man. 'Did you find it when you were travelling?'

'Yes, that's right,' said the traveller. 'I have seen the plant in many places.'

'What is this plant?' asked the rich man. 'I never heard about it until today.'

'Well, I saw the plant near this village,' said the young

At last, the young man stopped eating.

man. 'It grows at a place near here. Shall I take you there?'

'Yes! Please take me there!' said the rich man. He was very excited.

'Come with me,' said the young man. And he stood up.

'Wait!' said the rich man. 'Let's wait until it's dark. If we go now, everybody will know where the plant grows. It won't be a secret any longer.'

'All right,' said the traveller. He smiled. Then he sat down and he went to sleep.

The rich man waited and waited.

'Soon it will be dark,' he thought. 'Soon I'll learn the secret. The secret will make me very, very rich! Everybody will want the plant!'

At last, it was dark. The rich man woke the young traveller.

'Shall we go now?' he asked.

'Yes,' said the young man. 'Come with me!'

They left the rich man's house. They walked quietly through the village. It was very late. It was very dark. No one saw them. Everybody was asleep in their houses.

Soon the rich man and the traveller came to the rice field.

'There it is,' said the young man. He pointed to the fields of rice.

'Where? Where? I can't see it,' said the rich man.

'There!' said the young man.

'What do you mean, young man? Rice?' the rich man said angrily.

'Yes,' replied the traveller.

'Rice is the "wonderful plant"?' said the rich man.

'Yes, it is,' said the young man. 'Everywhere I travel, there is rice. Rice can feed all the people in a town or in a village. It can feed all the people in a city. Without rice, everybody would be hungry. When there is no other food, rice keeps people alive.'

The rich man was very angry. He had given this young man a good dinner!

The young man began to walk away.

'Well, goodbye, sir,' he said. 'I must go now. Thank you for my dinner. It was wonderful.'

And the young man quickly left the village.

After a few moments, the rich man began to smile. Then he began to laugh.

'Well, now I know the secret!' he said to himself. 'And the young man was right! Rice *is* a wonderful plant. It *does* feed everybody.'

Then he laughed again and he walked home.

Points for Understanding

WHY DUCKS SLEEP ON ONE LEG

1 Describe the ducks at the beginning of time.
2 What was the second duck's idea?
3 Who did the ducks go to see? Why?
4 What did he tell the ducks?
5 The ducks heard an angry voice.
  (a) What did the voice say?
  (b) Who did the ducks think this was?
6 Who was inside the temple? What did he do?
7 The ducks got their second legs.
  (a) Why were these legs special?
  (b) What promise did the ducks make?
8 What happens when ducks sleep?

THE KING OF HEAVEN'S UNCLE

1 What is a drought? Describe what happens.
2 Who went to see the King of Heaven?
3 The travellers got to the edge of the sea. How did they get to the gates of Heaven?
4 What did they hear?
5 What did the toad see in a large room?
6 What was the King of Heaven doing?
7 What did the toad think? What did he do? What did the King do next?
8 Who ran into the room?
9 Who did the toad call? What happened?
10 What frightened the dogs?
11 What made a noise louder than Thunder and Lightning?

12 What did the toad tell the King of Heaven about the Earth? What did the toad ask for?
13 What did the King of Heaven call the toad?
14 Who was the King of Heaven angry with? What did he tell them to do?
15 What do the Vietnamese people say about the toad?

THE SCHOLAR'S JOURNEY

1 What did the scholar want to be?
2 Had he been successful?
3 What troubles did the woodcutter's daughter have?
4 How could the scholar help?
5 Who did the scholar meet next? What was this person's trouble?
6 What did the scholar see at the river?
7 What trouble did he hear about?
8 How did the scholar cross the river?
9 The scholar told the gods about three of the troubles. What answers did he hear?
10 What did the scholar forget?
11 The scholar was given three things. What were they?
12 What did the scholar learn from his journey?

THE TWO IMMORTALS

1 Why did Tu Uyen not want to get married?
2 Tu Uyen went for a walk. What did he see, hear and smell?
3 Who did he see by the old pagoda? Describe this person.
4 Did Tu Uyen like this person? Give reasons for your answer.
5 The person suddenly went away. What did Tu Uyen think?

6 Tu Uyen had a dream. What happened in the dream?
7 Where did Tu Uyen go when he woke up? What did he see and do?
8 What did the servant put on the table? What did Tu Uyen put on the table?
9 Who was Giang Kieu? Where had she come from?
10 Giang Kieu told Tu Uyen to study his books. What was she going to do if he did not study?
11 What did Tu Uyen do every day and every night?
12 'I will kill myself.'
   Who said this? Why?
13 What happened when Tran Nhi was one year old?
14 What did Giang Kieu tell Tu Uyen?
15 Where did Tu Uyen and Giang Kieu go?
16 What did the villagers say about them? What did the villagers do?

THE CLEVER WIFE

1 The father of Hai and Ba died.
   (a) What did Hai have then?
   (b) What did Ba have?
2 Ba could not grow enough food.
   (a) What did he ask Hai?
   (b) What was the answer?
3 How was Hai's life different from Ba's life?
4 Hai's wife spoke to her husband about his friends. What did she say about them?
5 What did Hai's wife tell Hai that evening?
6 What was 'very heavy'? Why did Hai have to get help?
7 Hai visited his friends. Did the first two friends help him?
8 Who helped Hai?
9 How did the mandarin know what had happened?
10 What was in the blanket?
11 Hai's wife spoke to the mandarin. What did the mandarin do and say?

THE WONDERFUL PLANT

1 'Why are you smiling?' one of the villagers asked.
   What did the handsome young man reply?
2 What did the young traveller tell the villagers about?
3 Who wanted to meet the traveller?
4 What happened in this person's house?
5 What did the young man say about the wonderful plant?
6 The young man thought of a clever trick because he was
   hungry. Look back at the first two paragraphs of this
   story. There are two sentences which are clues to this
   trick. Which sentences are they?

ELEMENTARY LEVEL

A Christmas Carol *by Charles Dickens*
Riders of the Purple Sage *by Zane Grey*
The Canterville Ghost and Other Stories *by Oscar Wilde*
Lady Portia's Revenge and Other Stories *by David Evans*
The Picture of Dorian Gray *by Oscar Wilde*
Treasure Island *by Robert Louis Stevenson*
Road to Nowhere *by John Milne*
The Black Cat *by John Milne*
The Red Pony *by John Steinbeck*
The Stranger *by Norman Whitney*
Tales of Horror *by Bram Stoker*
Frankenstein *by Mary Shelley*
Silver Blaze and Other Stories *by Sir Arthur Conan Doyle*
Tales of Ten Worlds *by Arthur C. Clarke*
The Boy Who Was Afraid *by Armstrong Sperry*
Room 13 and Other Ghost Stories *by M.R. James*
The Narrow Path *by Francis Selormey*
The Lord of Obama's Messenger and Other Stories
by Marguerite Siek
Why Ducks Sleep on One Leg and Other Stories *by Anne Ingram*
The Gift From the Gods and Other Stories *by Anne Ingram*
The Land of Morning Calm and Other Stories *by Anne Ingram*
Love Conquers Death and Other Stories *by Catherine Khoo and Marguerite Siek*
The Stone Lion and Other Stories *by Claire Breckon*
The Bride of Prince Mudan and Other Stories *by Celine C. Hu*

For further information on the full selection of Readers at all five levels in the series, please refer to the Heinemann ELT Readers catalogue.

Macmillan Heinemann English Language Teaching, Oxford

A division of Macmillan Publishers Limited

Companies and representatives throughout the world

ISBN 0 435 27327 2

Heinemann is a registered trademark of Reed Educational & Professional Publishing Limited

These retold versions by John Escott for Heinemann Guided Readers
Text © Reed Educational and Professional Publishing Ltd 1997
Design and illustration
© Reed Educational and Professional Publishing Ltd 1997
First published 1997

Illustrated by Lee Kowling
Illustrations and map, pages 6 and 7, by John Gilkes
Typography by Sue Vaudin
Cover by Peter Goodfellow and Marketplace Design
Typeset in 11.5/14.5pt Goudy
Printed and bound in Spain by Mateu Cromo, S.A.

99   00 10   9   8   7   6   5   4   3